ANCHOR BOOKS/DOUBLEDAY

New York London Toronto

Sydney Auckland

KISSING GOD
GOODBYE

Poems

1991–1997

JUNE JORDAN

AN ANCHOR BOOK
PUBLISHED BY DOUBLEDAY
a division of Bantam Doubleday Dell Publishing Group, Inc.
1540 Broadway, New York, New York 10036

ANCHOR BOOKS, DOUBLEDAY, and the portrayal of an anchor are
trademarks of Doubleday, a division of Bantam Doubleday Dell
Publishing Group, Inc.

Book Design by Gretchen Achilles

Library of Congress Cataloging-in-Publication Data

Jordan, June, 1936–
   Kissing God goodbye: poems, 1991–1997 / June Jordan. — 1st
Anchor Books ed.
     p.   cm.
   I. Title.
PS3560.O73K57   1997
811'.54—dc21   97-18789
                                          CIP

ISBN 0-385-49032-1

FIRST ANCHOR BOOKS EDITION: NOVEMBER 1997
10 9 8 7 6 5 4 3 2 1

DEDICATION

$$4 \quad y^2$$

and

4 The Student Poet Revolutionaries
Alegría Barclay
Xochi Candelaria
Gary Chandler
Erwin Cho-Woods
Emily Derr
Jill Guerra
Rana Halpern
Dima Hilal
Aaron Jefferis
David Keiser
John Koo
Marisa Loeffen
Belinda Lyons
Maiana Minahal
Alison Peters
Laine Proctor
Marcos Ramírez
Shelly Teves
Marina Wilson
and
Debbie Walker (Datbu)
and
Junichi Semitsu

With my forever love and faith

v

Serious Thanks

to my (the beloved, the ace) literary agent,
Victoria Sanders
to my (the best, the brilliant) editor,
Janet Hill
to my (the consummate poet, the warrior) stalwart,
Sara Miles

and

to b.b.L.
for the homestead on the river

CONTENTS

KISSING GOD
GOODBYE

POEM FOR A YOUNG POET

Most people search all
of their lives
for someplace to belong to
as you said
but I look instead
into the eyes of anyone
who talks to me

I search for a face
to believe and belong to
a loosening mask
with a voice
ears
and a consciousness
breathing through
a nose
I can see

Day to day
it's the only way
I like to travel
noticing the colors of a cheek
the curvature of brow
and the public declarations
of two lips

Okay!
I did not say male
or female
I did not say Serbian
or Tutsi

I said
what tilts my head
into the opposite of fear
or dread
is anyone
who talks to me

A face
to claim or question
my next step away
or else towards

fifteen anemones
dilated well beyond apologics
for such an open centerpiece
that soft
forever begs for bees

one morning
and the birdsong and the dew-
struck honeysuckle blending
invitations to dislodge
my fingers tangling with my sunlit
lover's hair

A face
to spur or interdict
my mesmerized approach
or else
my agonized reproach

to strangulations of the soul
that bring a mother
to disown
her children

leaving them alone to feed
on bone and dust

A face
despite a corpse
invasion of the cradle
where I rock my love
alive

A face
despite numb fashions
of an internet connection between nobody
and no one

A face
against the narcoleptic/antiseptic
chalk streaks
in the sky
that lie
and posit credit cards
and starched de facto exposés
as copacetic evidence
that you and I
need no defense
against latrine
and bully bullet-proof decisions
launched by limousines
dividing up the big screen
into gold points
cold above the valley
of the shadow of unpardonable
tiny
tiny
tiny
this breathing and that breath

and then
that and that
that death

I search a face
a loosening mask
with voice
ears
and a consciousness
breathing through
a nose
that I can see

I search a face
for obstacles to genocide
I search beyond the dead
and
driven by imperfect visions
of the living
yes and no
I come and go
back to the eyes
of anyone
who talks to me

dedicated to
Erwin Cho-Woods
May 27, 1997

NOVEMBER POEM FOR ALEGRÍA: 1996

I have seen concrete
disintegrate
under the weight of water

I have seen stone and steel
yield
to students
civil
disobedient
and fasting
and lasting
open to the rain

And goodbye to the men
and goodbye to the women
angry at the wind
frightened by the bright light
horrified by strangers

Goodbye!
Goodbye!

I have heard
the tender speaking
of many tongues

I have heard
the breaking voice beg

Here ends civility
Now we know the strategy of stars

continuous
exempt from tinkering
and beyond numerical reduction

Now we know the strategy of trees
that flourish
roots protected or exposed
above the famished
or the flooded
earth
and lifting
always
lifting up the air
itself

No more polishing of pain!

Here ends surrender:

I have seen the face
of every promise from the sun

I have seen the bestial
kneel
beside the bodies of young poets
standing
in your tears

WHAT GREAT GRIEF HAS MADE THE EMPRESS MUTE

NY Times Headline

Because it was raining outside the palace
Because there was no rain in her vicinity

Because people kept asking her questions
Because nobody ever asked her anything

Because marriage robbed her of her mother
Because she lost her daughters to the same tradition

Because her son laughed when she opened her mouth
Because he never delighted in anything she said

Because romance carried the rose inside a fist
Because she hungered for the fragrance of the rose

Because the jewels of her life did not belong to her
Because the glow of gold and silk disguised her soul

Because nothing she could say could change the melted
    music of her space
Because the privilege of her misery was something she could
    not disgrace

Because no one could imagine reasons for her grief
Because her grief required no imagination

Because it was raining outside the palace
Because there was no rain in her vicinity

Dedicated to The Empress Michiko

and to

Janice Mirikitani

ARGUMENT WITH THE BUDDHA

We agree
about the suffering
disease
decrepitude
and incremental
death

or
nobody hold the child
nobody bless the scar
nobody change the meaning
of the land
     the regular
insensibility of trying to farm
the rocks
     trying to beg a meal
from shadow offerings
of your body
     trying to reduce the craziness
of motion without trace

We disagree
about desire

I own a whole address book
full of names and numbers
I no longer care about
and the moral of that story
     contradicts (in sum)
The wisdom of whoever forgets
to want somebody else

alive and troublesome
despite the slide
towards sleep
I need new names!

And I have never done one single thing
for 49 days straight
much less to sit myself beneath some tree
And no one entertains
me
with ten thousand dancing
girls/
a feast of fruit and fresh
killed
curry lamb
or jewels strewn across my table
top

So I renounce
renunciation!

This hand that writes
and waits
and writes and waits
again
These ears that listen
for the rain
or wind that catapults
the tree
into a standing hazard

ignorant of roots

I choose and cherish
all that will perish
The living deal

The balance of my bliss
with pain

excites my soul

perhaps to no enlightenment
but

rather than transcend
what makes me ache

I hope to fend
off enemies
and bend with
lovers
endlessly

I choose
anything
anyone
I may lose

I renounce
renunciation

I breathe
head to head
with suffering

and after that

nothing
for sure

dedicated to
Shelly Teves
2/15/96 Berkeley

merry-go-round poetry

For one second there
you lay your face against
the brass
support on which the earth
turned high and low
a carousel of horse and rider
in electrical affinity
and I saw
that pole become like melted gold
impressionable and precious
from that momentary contact
with the reckless
question
of your cheek
and I knew the music of your rising
through the air
would not subside
or disappear

LEBANON
LEBANON

I

Faces I have never seen before
language I have never heard
before
        between me
        and the enemy
the difference blurred
by blood
dried
only yesterday

(I would have loved to walk beside the sand
the turquoise water
tickling at the fingers of my idle
hand)

this amputation of my tongue
this clotted artery that starts
a fatal stuttering

this massacre
I photograph
the withered aftermath
the oozing consequence
the swollen stump
the burned out cranial configuration
of a 6 year old
recovering

from abrupt incineration
of her dress her hair
her plastic daisy bracelet singed
into a 3rd degree
tattoo
        do I exaggerate?
or not
recovering

and shrunken to a charcoal
junked life shifted
into shadows
upon shadows of the shadows
fire borne
the lasting flash
outlasts
the leaking
scar
become
a relic
of its breathing
minimum

Or how shall I collect
the rubble of the landscape/
flesh smell
on the floor

or cave containers
of the throat
that livid
howls
a huge hole
in the house wall

fallen loose
the left
leg blown away
below
the howling
livid
knee
or how will I begin
to guarantee a denudation
to the bone of knowing
from
the meat of bodies
of the howling
livid
one eye
shot to pieces
two eyes
shot to pieces
of the meat
of the shattering
of the rain
of the bodies
howling
livid

how

II

I would have loved
I would
I would
I would have

water of one glass
passing
hand to hand
the ceremony of the stacked-up
fotos of the no more
no more mother no
more mother's
mother's
son
no father no
more no
more
from one to twenty four
no more no
village family
still
alive

I would have loved
I would
I would
I would have
        touched the buttons of his shirt
        traced my longing light
        along his shoulders

how
does he survive

this hospital
this public bed
these daily saviors
without name
        his bearded face
        as beautiful

as hushed
his everlasting tilted
stare
as liquid
as deliberate
as deep

as what will he
never say

as what will he
never see

again

without that blasted
limb
exploded from its socket

blasted
taken without anesthesia
or amnesia

I would have loved
I would
I would
I would have loved
          what he will never see
          again

III

As usual
I have to ask

where's Jesus
when you need him

The miracle of water into wine's
just fine
but what about
a miracle of blood
delivering a river
we can drink

IV

behold the woolly lamb
beside the children
shivering
in shock

behold the refugees
aroused by soap
and blankets
(maybe
blankets)

behold a people
lost inside the landscape
that belongs to them
behold a landscape
taken by the fiend
of force

v

How do you evacuate
a country?

offshore
the gunboats have begun
the shelling
of the highway
and the houses

above
the orange groves
the f-16's drop
death

and from a balding hilltop
only eyeball meters'
distant from a field
of rusted car parts
dissolute among wild
flowers
trusting all that color from the sun
artillery
destroys the heated laughter
of another
lost
civilian afternoon

Lebanon
Lebanon

the mountain of the people of the mountain

Lebanon
Lebanon

the cedar trees forever foraging the air
for earth for space
for non-negotiable longevity

Lebanon
Lebanon

the sea refusing to recede
the open sky that will not blink
the wailing of the soul that does not sleep
the worry beads that spell
    apocalypse specific to this man
    this woman

Lebanon
Lebanon

the 12 year old who sings aloud
to calm the other children
terrified by murder

Here do I discover
the humility
the miracle of suffering
without surrender
the miracle of suffering
without defeat

dedicated to the people of Lebanon

and to Laura

SHORT TAKES

I

Somebody works up a sweat
in the vineyard
I drive by

II

I am not your East coast weather
cyclical
and always coming
back
in your direction

III

Those grapes!
Growing in such straight rows!
Who will savor
the smell and the flavor
(the madness)
of all that wine!

IV

Leaves loosening lost
your or my eyes turned away
this spiral spins slow

SOMETIMES CLARITY COMES IN THE DARK

I turn my body to the side
where formerly you lay
asleep
or whispering
or hot
where you are not
now
or ever
close
to me

POEM AFTER RECEIVING VOICEMAIL FROM YOU AFTER (I DON'T EVEN KNOW ANYMORE) HOW LONG!

Your voice and the weighted
stammering between us
evident
and the train of my routine
adjustment to nothing anywhere
as unforgettable
as your bare feet on the flagstone
pathway
next to bunched up honeysuckle
blooming aromatic in the a.m.
of a daily life
we shared but never dared
to lock and key
into
our problematic/
intersection—
That train derailed/my
regular defenses failed
to lower the volume
of the million and one
or zero
meanings
of your call

TANKA TRIO

I

Fallen on the street
Black woman wrestling with air
Bloody hair and teeth
No small change in her pockets
Big change always pass her by

II

El campesino
stoops all day above the dirt
strawberries flourish
strange wages for sweat and strain
Darkness cover him with rain

III

What I need right now
after the rising water
What I need right now
after the pounding collapse
body surf a new wave fast

GHAFLAH

(In Islam, *Ghaflah* refers to the sin of forgetfulness)

Grief scrapes at my skin
she never
"Be a big girl!"
wanted to touch
much
except to disinfect
or bandage

I acknowledge nothing

I forget the mother of my hurt
her innocence of pride
her suicide

That first woman

lowered eyes
folded hands
withered limbs
among the plastic flowers
rhinestone bracelets
eau de toilette
trinkets from slow
compromise

Where did she go?

After swallowing fifteen/twenty/thirty-five pills
she tried to rise
and rising

froze
forever trying to arise
from compromise

And I do not remember finding her
like that
half seated half
almost standing up
just dead
by her own hand
just dead

I do not remember finding her
like that

I forget the burned toast/
spinach
cold eggs
taste-free tuna fish
and thin spread peanut butter
sandwiches
she left for me

I erase
the stew the soup
she cooked and carried
everywhere
to neighbors

I forget three or four other things
I cannot recall
how many pairs of pretty shoes
how many dressup overcoats
I saved my nickels
dimes and quarters

all year long
to buy
at Christmas time
to give to her
my mother
she
the one who would wear nothing
beautiful

Or how I strut
beside her walking anywhere
prepared for any lunatic
assault
upon her shuffling
journey
to a bus stop

I acknowledge nothing

I forget she taught me
how to pray
I forget her prayers
And mine

I do not remember
kneeling down
to ask for wisdom
high-top sneakers
or linoleum chips
to animate
my zip gun

I have never remembered
the blistering fury
the abyss

into which
I capsized
after her last
compromise

I wish I had found her
that first woman
my mother
trying to rise
up

I wish I had given her
my arm

both arms

I have never forgiven her
for going away

But I don't remember anything

Grief scrapes at my skin
she never
"Be a big girl!"
wanted to touch
much

HAIKU FOR THE WOULD-BE KILLERS OF A TEACHER

You cut down that tree
Tore off the new leaves and left
Roots to bless that dirt

dedicated to Janet Hill

BRIDGET SONG #1

Late in the day and near
a growing edge of redwood
trees
and following a solitary
trail
I saw you/fern
ravine nirvana
passing by

but then you changed
direction
and came back
to walk with me

and I will never be
the same

Before you knew my name
I knew
nobody treads the earth
as close
as light
as you

And I am turned around
because
the ceremony of your movement
slides along
the shadow of a shining
sound

STUDY #1

Let me be
very
very
very
very
very
specific

Let me not forget about
or
Let me not forget about
anything like
anything like
an eyelash
lost above your lips

When the President says no to legislation
to make cocaine more criminal like crack
or crack less criminal like cocaine
so that white men as well as black
get nailed for jail

When the President says no
When the President says no
When the President says no to Fidel Castro
When the President talks about Human Rights
and moral guiding lights and then
The President says yes
to a total mess of multi-multi-
millionfold
marketplace

potentate
Toms and Dicks and Harrys and then
And then when the President
says no to Fidel Castro

Let me be
very
very
very
very
very
specific

The criminal inertia
The criminal morality of inertia
The criminal morality of inertia nothing
nothing
nothing
not even the junked baby tied to the chair
not even the smashed face woman
        dragged through the house by
                what's left of her hair

nothing
nothing
interdicts
the criminal inertia
of suit and tie/
or my
complacency

Nothing
Nothing
Not even the beautiful man
parking my car or

sweeping the airport terminal floor
only because so far no
robot can
absolutely replace a beautiful man
while unemployment and huge profits rise
amid official spokesmanly lies
about the no jobs future
we're definitely due for

Nothing
Nothing interdicts
the criminal inertia
of suit and tie
or my
complacency

Or let me not forget
Or let me not forget about 2 miles
below my house
a train moves
moaning through the night
(I said:) 2 miles below my house
a train moves
moaning through the night

Let me be
very
very
very
very
very
specific
Now that the U.S. Congress agrees
That nobody American
has a right to anything besides

acute emotional
    physical
    and economic
    anxieties

Let me be
very
very
very
very
very
specific

Let me not forget about
or
Let me not forget about
anything like
anything like
an eyelash
lost above your lips

(please baby please)

THE ECLIPSE OF 1996

Everybody out of the house!
Everybody up on the roof!
Run to the top of the street!
Pull back the branches of the trees!
Abandon all cars!
Do you hear me?
Bring the children!
Carry your babies into the night!
THE LIGHT'S ABOUT TO GO OUT!
We've finally managed to shut down the shining of the
    moon!

And you wouldn't want
to miss that

wouldya?

MESSAGE FROM BELFAST
FOR JUSTICE AND FOR GERRY ADAMS

At 4 A.M.
I imagine you somewhere safe
and sunny
and I pray that you stay there
far away from here
where I watch for the daring
of dawn and men
again on these dangerous
streets
way below the window
of my lovely most-blown-up-hotel-
in-Europe
room
where I pace with cigarettes
and a useless telephone
trying to last through the night

From half a mile away
I see
that stacked slum
high-rise
concrete monstrosity
where Catholic families
crumble from a cruel
chronic surveillance
exercised
by British teenage soldiers
spilling loose on the sidewalk
assault rifles cocked
while they stalk backwards

into plastic toys and tricycles
and children
blown apart
the papers say
by accident

And in-between my untouched bed
and the kitchen chaos
of such incendiary
occupation
I see
railroad tracks but no trains
I see
one highway overpass
carrying no traffic
I smell blood
but I see
none of the bodies
buried close to each other
father/brother
son

This afternoon
the car grew dark before my eyes
and I looked up and up and up
into the towering
effrontery of a British tank
parked
killer casual
across the corner of a street
of homes so humble
this one intrusion
smashed the sanctuary purpose
of the neighborhood
I began to eat my notes

I began to make comparisons to police
in Harlem or the Nicaragua contras
I began to stop bothering about comparisons
I began to count each close and opening of my eyes
each proof of breath not death
            among my friends
            not one of us
            shot down
            dragged out and beaten
            or "detained"
            indefinitely
            without charge
            or tortured
            without recourse
            for however long some military sadist
            might find imperial
            abuse
            amusing

I thought, "This might be it—
(around and behind
ubiquitous combat boots
a foreign Army flagrant
with
its lockstep slur in front of church
or posing on a housing project
wall with SLR and SA-80 semi-
automatic rifles
eager
to go off—
This heavy thread through heavy terror
for a secret cup
of tea
and hands across an oil cloth covered

tabletop)
This might be it"

And listening to the stories
and the songs
of all my comrades
bickering/hilarious and loud
and anticipating (any
minute) the explosion
that would blast
our whole thing
into a statistical
addition
to "The Troubles"

I thought
This has always been
the deal: The danger
The derogation of my image of my gods
The enemy invasion
The tank on the cobblestone
The tip of the bayonet puncturing your skin
The bullet longing for your very best flesh

Well
it rained for 20 minutes
and a rainbow
gorged its colors from the gun gray weather
of this Irish no-man's zone

This city is so small
You could never murder anybody
by mistake
And there is not a playground to be found

for all the babies
—Only War—

I am afraid to fall
asleep
but I am proud
to stand before the morning
breaks
awake with no one near
and with my conscience clear
for once
I am completely where
I ought to be

In the city
of Belfast
I have lost and found myself
at home

LETTER TO MRS. VIRGINIA THOMAS, WIFE OF WHATZHISNAME LAMENTABLY APPOINTED TO THE SUPREME COURT, U.S.A.

And here I thought I hated him!
I mean I thought that he was loathsome to the nth
degree
I saw him as some kinda clown
a first class
colored fool
an Uncle Tom
a Peeping Tom
a creepy eager pornographic Tom
a hypocrite
a liar and a fake
a make-
believe Black man
a mediocre mediocrity of apple polish
brown nose cut-throat
and an insult to his elders
a menace to his peers
a hazard to the under seventeen
a joke
a serious mistake
a cynical disjuncture between race
and history
a cruel interlocutor between the needy
and relief
a bullet to the family
a bully to the female
a pietistic turncoat
and a trivializing renegade
a jerk

a cornball hustler and a trifling no 'count crocodile
a sacrilegious opportunist
and a hitman for the pitiless

But
I'm completely off the track/ mistaken/ out of line and
off the wall
(it seems)
which brings me to this letter I must write to you:
I write to thank you for your revelation!
I declare
I don't know how
the truth escaped my understanding
I can't explain the blindness that concealed
the facts
from me

But suddenly
I looked at you and Clarence
happy as 2 pods in a poke (or 2 pigs in a pea or
whatever)
on the cover of *People* Magazine
and things just clicked
They really did!
I mean like *click:*
I realized you're right
and I been dense and dumb and bigtime
into criminal denial
see
because
I probably was
(as you say) probably I was
in love with Clarence!
Probably I lusted after him/ your husband:
Yes I guess

I probably did!
And here I thought I hated him!
But then
you never know:
Sometimes it's awful hard to tell
now isn't it:

You never know!

FIRST POEM AFTER SERIOUS SURGERY

The breath continues but the breathing
hurts
Is this the way death wins its way
against all longing
and redemptive thrust from grief?
Head falls
Hands crawl
and pain becomes the only keeper
of my time

I am not held
I do not hold
And touch degenerates into new
agony

I feel
the healing of cut muscle/
broken nerves
as I return to hot and cold
sensations
of a body tortured by the flight
of feeling/normal
registrations of repulsion
or delight

On this meridian of failure or recovery
I move
or stop respectful
of each day
but silent now
and slow

THE BOMBING OF BAGHDAD

I

began and did not terminate for 42 days
and 42 nights relentless minute after minute
more than 110,000 times
we bombed Iraq we bombed Baghdad
we bombed Basra/we bombed military
installations we bombed the National Museum
we bombed schools we bombed air raid
shelters we bombed water we bombed
electricity we bombed hospitals we
bombed streets we bombed highways
we bombed everything that moved/we
bombed everything that did not move we
bombed Baghdad
a city of 5.5 million human beings
we bombed radio towers we bombed
telephone poles we bombed mosques
we bombed runways we bombed tanks
we bombed trucks we bombed cars we bombed bridges
we bombed the darkness we bombed
the sunlight we bombed them and we
bombed them and we cluster bombed the citizens
of Iraq and we sulfur bombed the citizens of Iraq
and we napalm bombed the citizens of Iraq and we
complemented these bombings/these "sorties" with
Tomahawk cruise missiles which we shot
repeatedly by the thousands upon thousands
into Iraq
(you understand an Iraqi Scud missile

is *quote* militarily insignificant *unquote* and we
do not mess around with insignificant)
so we used cruise missiles repeatedly
we fired them into Iraq
And I am not pleased
I am not very pleased
None of this fits into my notion of "things going very
      well"

II

The bombing of Baghdad
did not obliterate the distance or the time
between my body and the breath
of my beloved

III

This was Custer's Next-To-Last Stand
I hear Crazy Horse singing as he dies
I dedicate myself to learn that song
I hear that music in the moaning of the Arab world

IV

Custer got accustomed to just doing his job
Pushing westward into glory
Making promises
Searching for the savages/their fragile
temporary settlements
for raising children/dancing down the rain/and praying

for the mercy of a herd of buffalo
Custer/he pursued these savages
He attacked at dawn
He murdered the men/murdered the boys
He captured the women and converted
them (I'm sure)
to his religion
Oh, how gently did he bid his darling fiancee
farewell!
How sweet the gaze her eyes bestowed upon her warrior!
Loaded with guns and gunpowder he embraced
the guts and gore of manifest white destiny
He pushed westward
to annihilate the savages
("Attack at dawn!")
and seize their territories
   seize their women
   seize their natural wealth

V

And I am cheering for the arrows
and the braves

VI

And all who believed some must die
they were already dead
And all who believe only they possess
human being and therefore human rights
they no longer stood among the possibly humane
And all who believed that retaliation/revenge/defense

derive from God-given prerogatives of white men
And all who believed that waging war is anything
     besides terrorist activity in the first
     place and in the last
And all who believed that F-15's/F-16's/"Apache"
     helicopters/
B-52 bombers/smart bombs/dumb bombs/napalm/artillery/
battleships/nuclear warheads amount to anything other
than terrorist tools of a terrorist undertaking
And all who believed that holocaust means something
     that happens only to white people
And all who believed that Desert Storm
     signified anything besides the delivery of an American
     holocaust against the peoples of the Middle East
All who believed these things
they were already dead
They no longer stood among the possibly humane

And this is for Crazy Horse singing as he dies
because I live inside his grave
And this is for the victims of the bombing of Baghdad
because the enemy traveled from my house
        to blast your homeland
        into pieces of children
        and pieces of sand

And in the aftermath of carnage
perpetrated in my name
how should I dare to offer you my hand
how shall I negotiate the implications
        of my shame?

My heart cannot confront
this death without relief

My soul will not control
this leaking of my grief

And this is for Crazy Horse singing as he dies
And here is my song of the living
who must sing against the dying
sing to join the living
with the dead

OCTOBER SNOWPEA POEM

So as the sun declines below Detroit
(the lake a cool
assurance of alternatives to hard
dark high-rise
miscellaneous)
the colors of the end of light
relax along the horizontal edge of this
blue place
with burnt sienna
rose and oranges
that soften into regular
domestic tragedies
of night
without a lover's willing
face
to stop the desperation of the chase
for daytime stars
that glint and blur and mix and lift
like mica sprinkling
on a concrete hieroglyph of altered space
where
by himself
a young black man
sits
still

for no good reason

so do I turn to memorize
the soft excitement of the homestretch of your lips

and close to the hypnosis
of your almost closing eyes
I spin to the surprise
of no pain/no pain
whatsoever

CAMPSITE #21
for Y²

Next to so many stars
next to a meadow of wild oats rising to dry
next to a barrel full of flame and remnants of flame
next to the water bubbling full of rice
next to the knives
next to the feast of the wooden skewers
next to the roasted mushrooms/onion/shrimp and chunks
    of ripe red pepper
next to the wine and the cooler and the candle and
    the flashlights
next to the gigantic redwood tree
next to the mountains receding but never
    shadowy or lost
next to the very spot where Venus
    blinked delirious as I felt close
        enough to feel the Milky Way
    collapse into the aerial Big
    Dipper poised above our bodies
    close enough to feel
    our bodies close
        together

2½ miles up
from the beginning of the forest
2½ miles up
from the ending of a regular road
pretty damn high
after
tying knots

of white nylon to aluminum
stakes
or bending bamboo poles
into the pockets
of our borrowed tent
or shooing our ground
away from possible killer
ants
but next to squirrels and a curious
raccoon
soon you were blowing on the fire
and sparks burst from the dark
few inches left
between us
like the incandescent tremor
of a moon
that will not spoil an expectation
with its full disclosure

Next to you
the 2 blue sleeping bags
zipped tight
together
and I felt the lifted
lifting
positive security of a well-made
kite

and I felt the irresistible
the naked nature of the right
enclosure

       your handiwork
       your arms

around me

while the lone hawk of the evening
he forgot about the hungers
of the sun

and glided by

BOSNIA BOSNIA

Too bad
there is no oil
between her legs

that 4-year-old Muslim girl and
her 5-year-old sister
and the 16-year-old babysitter
and the 20-year-old mother of that 4-year-old/that
Muslim child gang raped
from dawn to dark to time become damnation

Too bad
there is no oil
between her legs

Too bad there is no oil
between Sbrenica and Sarajevo
and in-between the standing of a life
and genocide

Too bad
there is no oil

Too bad
there is no oil
between her legs

the woman in Somalia
who weighs 45 pounds and
who has buried village elders and
who has buried village children

who weighed even less
than she weighs after so many days
of hunger gaping open
to the flies

Too bad
there is no oil
in South Central L.A.
and in between the beaten men and beatup women
and in between the African and Asian throwaways
and in between the Spanish and the English speaking
homeless
and in between the dealers and the drugged
and in between the people and criminal police
too bad
there is no oil

Too bad
there is no oil
between her legs
that four-year-old Muslim girl

Too bad
there is no oil
between her legs

FOCUS IN REAL TIME

A bowl of rice
        as food
        as politics
        or metaphor
        as something valuable and good
        or something common to consume/exploit/ignore

Who grew these grains
Who owned the land
Who harvested the crop
Who converted these soft particles to money
Who kept the cash
Who shipped the consequences of the cash
Who else was going to eat the rice
Who else was going to convert the rice to cash

Who would design the flowers for the outside of the bowl
Who would hold the bowl between her hands
Who would give the bowl away
Who could share the rice
Who could fill that bowl with rice how many times a day
                how many times a week
Who would adore the hands that held the bowl that held
   the rice
Who would adore the look the smell the steam of boiled
   rice
               in a bowl

Who will analyze the cash the rice becomes
Who will sit beside the bowl or fight for rice

Who will write about the hands that hold the bowl
Who will want to own the land
        A bowl of rice

poem for **MARGARET**

who passed the California Bar!

POEM IN MEMORY OF ALAN SCHINDLER, 22 YEARS OLD

Except for the tattoo
how could I recognize
my son
what with the way that monster
crushed
his skull
what with the way that monster
broke
then pulverized his jaw
what with the way that monster
kicked apart
the rib cage of my only son/
except for the tattoo
how could I recognize
my boy
my manchild grown into a sailor
for the Navy

I have buried him
my son
who lived and died loving
other men
I have buried him now
beneath the earth that allows for no
distinctions among men
except for the tattoo
that personal flag
of an honest body
as courageous
as ordinary

as continuing to breathe
when the world demands your death
as courageous
as ordinary
as an everyday parade
across mined territory
as courageous
as ordinary
as all of that
except
Thank God!
except for the tattoo

POEM BECAUSE THE 1996 U.S. POET LAUREATE TOLD THE *SAN FRANCISCO CHRONICLE* THERE ARE "OBVIOUS" POETS— ALL OF THEM WHITE—AND THEN THERE ARE "REPRESENTATIVE" POETS—NONE OF THEM WHITE

So the man said
Let there be obvious people
and representative others.
Let there be obvious poets
and representative
others
Let the obvious people be white
Let the others
represent what happens
when
you fail to qualify
as obvious

And the representative other
not obvious people or poets
worried a lot about just what should you do
if you fall into
such a difficult
such a representative
slot

Except for one representative
sista poet
who said, "Mista
Poet Laureate!
Please clarify:
Was Timothy McVeigh

was he
obvious?

And what about media experts
certain that the murdering terrorist
must look like somebody, 'Middle
Eastern'?
Would you say that expertise was
representative?

And how about the cops trying to stop
then
trying to kill
Rodney King?

And Sheriff's deputies
Racing to vilify
and humiliate
Twenty-one Mexican men and women wannabe
working for minimum
wages
in America/how
about those
deputies who chose
on camera
to vent the venom
of their obvious
territorial assertions over land
that (truth to tell)
belongs to Mexico?

How about all histories
of all the deputies
hellbent to freeze inverted boundaries
according to some Anglo-Saxon
Christian
English Speaking

Crock of Conquest-As-The-Best
of-Destinies?
And Patrick Buchanan!

Is he obvious?
Is he legal?

That no way
alien
neo-nazi wannabe
neo-nazi 'über alles'
promising death to 'José'
and to *Niggas Jews* and *Queers*
That obvious
clear
leader
for obvious
clear
people
would you say
he's the bees' knees'
representative?"

Yes?
No?

Not all of us must come and go
by pick-up truck
And you can't yank each one
of us
right off the driver's seat
to beat up
on our heads and bloody backs!

And after twisted kicks
and billy sticks
to knock us down to

knock us down
to ground
our fathers and our mothers
sanctified/sweat
laboring to escape
the leather whip
you label who
illegal
or unqualified?

And dangerous to standards
and a way of life
that venerates brutality
and turns around to smirk
with overt
obvious
and homicidal
pride
you label who
illegal?

And burrowing under everything you think
you know
some of us move slow
like inch worms
softening the earth
to bury you

And how I hope the obvious
necessity for me to write
this poem
Translates into Spanish
Mandarin
Cantonese
Punjabi

Japanese
Xhosa
Arabic

and every African
and every Asian
language

Of every people representative
of people
kept unequal
on the planet

Mista
Poet Laureate
I close this disquisition
on the obvious
with the words of representative
Poet Hero
Langston Hughes:

"The night is beautiful
so the faces of my people

The stars are beautiful
so the eyes of my people

Beautiful, also, is the sun.
Beautiful, also, are the souls
        of my people."[1]

dedicated to Laura Serna

[1] "My People," by Langston Hughes from *Selected Poems*, Langston Hughes, Vintage Books, 1974, p. 13.

poem to continue a conversation
for Erwin Cho-Woods

changing through the day
or night
        words never stay the same
sounds bounding to a brain
without my mouth

        old syllables
aim
away from the light
        the revelations
of a glance
        or gaze
confound
        statistical inequities
like zero
        this kind of a life
        or that
blueberries
buffalo
        nothing anywhere
        extinct

if you if I
if we
just
face it

CHRISTMAS POEM
dedicated to the one and only Adrienne B. Torf

I

Clouds flying across the sky
and the moon
and the moon
and I hold
still

II

All that milky light full
enough to push and pull
the open sea
and lull that tipsy trickster
to her knees

III

And around
the infinite surf
and the sound
of its infinite pounding
little else
besides two yellow breasted sugar birds
domestic
among jasmine murmurs

IV

And how
the lone blue heron
stands
wherever
wherever it lands

POEM AT THE END OF THE THIRD YEAR

Free from an earlier debility
an almost ultimate commotion
in the opening mouth of death
I pass by Kezar stadium
where you spent our Sundays
Running
no strain
just speed and gaining stamina
as graceful as the lazy
sunlight boiling up
the air

How we began
a galaxy apart/me
driving on this street
to reach the hospital to take
away one breast
or more
than that

You arriving on this street
to take
and take again
the track
to pre-Olympic competition
training
training
hard and fast as heartbreak

Useless to each other
then and now
except the difference
kept me
keeps me
going

BIRTHDAY IN PARIS

Move the buffalo

bird close to its boundless eye

weight and wings one face

for Peter Sellars
September 27, 1995

STUDY #2 FOR b.b.L.

so you're gone
going
away
gone

And I never thought I'd jump
And I never thought you'd deal

And now
And now
And now

You're gone
going
away
gone

         gone
         go
         going away
         gone
ohwellohwellohwell
and the last of the clearing of the skies
and the last of my face inside your eyes

      away
   going away
away

Baby, Baby I
what can I say

I
I disappear
        away
        going away gone
from the tease me possibilities
from the going
from the going away gone

possibilities

of your tongue

And I never thought I'd jump
and I never thought you'd deal

but now
but now

           come back
           come back back
           here
           to my
           everything I
           I disappear
           without/back/here

ohwellohwellohwelloh
flying lowdown slip
flow
skip
baby
baby
so you're gone!

what can I where can I
what
without you

why would I what could I
what
without you/you're
what I what
would I
do
without
do
without
you
so you're gone
going away gone
and I don't care
I don't
        I don't care
        you're gone
        I don't care
        you're gone
        I don't care
And now

I need you back
here
I need you back
here
I need you back
here
in my
in my
in my
I need you back

here
in my
everything I
I disappear
without you

back here

going
away
gone

so you're gone
ohwellohwellohwellohwell

I need you back!

POEM #1 FOR b.b.L.

5 months
eighteen days
three dinners
three countries
two transatlantic
two trans-Mediterranean
flights
one hundred trans-continental
e-mail messages
seven or eight Fed Ex deliveries
four or five letters
2 bowls of granola
146 phone calls
2X playing tennis
one walk
one drive
one salt water
one fresh water
swim
2 hotels
4 or 5 tapes
3 or 4 photographs
one taxi
two books
one movie
and some bimbo
asking me
what's the plan?
one/two/three/four/five months
18 days
3 dinners

spinning into one winner word
like "DUCK!"
that heedless
downy
feathered
thing

that one word
heedless
downy
feathered
three countries
2 transatlantic
okay
okay
so maybe
that's the plan?

POEM #3 FOR b.b.L.

volcanic particles
between the moon and me
looking for a blue
moon
or a new
moon
or any kind of soon
moon
snuff the particles and stuff
the blues back
where no cold
turkey catch a hold
on me
from fingertips
to nipples
quivering
for some macroscopic
I mean incontrovertible
I mean beyond atomic
    and below the subcutaneous
    and above the epithelial
    and diaphanous (for sure)
    but pedestrian as sweat
    and local like your skin
    taking in
    the/evidence
    baby
    hardcore
    no metaphor
    evidence
    I mean proof

superluminal
exploding
proof
baby
evidence of incendiary
closeup particles
volcanic
like a true blue love

FACT SHEETS FOR b.b.L

No matter how I dawdle
or delay
you do not stay tonight
where only hours ago
you lay
not quite asleep
and close enough
for love
      (to keep)

POEM #4 FOR b.b.L.

At this beach where the water
rolled emerald as grass
infused by noonday light
and where you could forget
about the sky
because the ocean strayed
left right
forward
forward
hurtling always soft
into a last turn surf
we played
on these striated cliffs
strewn now and then
with rocks
or boulders
hard to touch
but never holding hard
against
your lifted weight
and then this game
of break
this rock
(okay)
then break this bigger
one
(okay)
and then
(okay)
this mountain bit
just try it

and it broke
it crumbled
and it pulverized
to cooling granules
you could shift
about
and sift
for gold
you had to hope nobody else
would notice

Then we raced towards that almost avalanche
that steep/
that risen
sand/we
jumped
and landed
dug-in
hot and staring
at a day
so bright so big
nothing
no one could obliterate
the look
the laughter
of the waves
your lips
precipitate

POEM FOR LAURA

Light as the almond tree petals
cherish each inch
of a solar infusion
that swells into color
and smell

Light as the traveling of land
beyond measure by miles
or the speed of delivery
from need

Light as the infinite wick
of a tiger's eye
kindling its own
appetite

Light as the call against stop
diminishing or dead
to obfuscate
the way to homestead
on the river

Light as the river

Light

POEM #6 FOR b.b.L.

One room away you sleep or do not wake
to any summons love might make
in competition with all hummingbirds/
those wings of utmost stutter
at the starting source
for rapture

infinitesimal
I take away the noise the words
that might disturb
or curb
your flight
and think how you will
curling
pearl into the night
with all my world
at stake

POEM #7 FOR b.b.L.

Baby
when you reach out
for me
I forget everything
except
I do try to remember
to breathe

INTIFADA INCANTATION:
POEM #8 FOR b.b.L.

I SAID I LOVED YOU AND I WANTED
GENOCIDE TO STOP
I SAID I LOVED YOU AND I WANTED AFFIRMATIVE
ACTION AND REACTION
I SAID I LOVED YOU AND I WANTED MUSIC
OUT THE WINDOWS
I SAID I LOVED YOU AND I WANTED
NOBODY THIRST AND NOBODY
NOBODY COLD
I SAID I LOVED YOU AND I WANTED I WANTED
JUSTICE UNDER MY NOSE
I SAID I LOVED YOU AND I WANTED
BOUNDARIES TO DISAPPEAR

I WANTED
NOBODY ROLL BACK THE TREES!
I WANTED
NOBODY TAKE AWAY DAYBREAK!
I WANTED
NOBODY FREEZE ALL THE PEOPLE ON THEIR
KNEES!

I WANTED YOU
I WANTED YOUR KISS ON THE SKIN OF MY SOUL
AND NOW YOU SAY YOU LOVE ME AND I STAND
DESPITE THE TRILLION TREACHERIES OF SAND
YOU SAY YOU LOVE ME AND I HOLD THE LONGING
OF THE WINTER IN MY HAND
YOU SAY YOU LOVE ME AND I COMMIT

TO FRICTION AND THE UNDERTAKING
OF THE PEARL

YOU SAY YOU LOVE ME
YOU SAY YOU LOVE ME

AND I HAVE BEGUN
I BEGIN TO BELIEVE MAYBE
MAYBE YOU DO

I AM TASTING MYSELF
IN THE MOUTH OF THE SUN

TANKA METAPHORS OR NOT FOR
b.b.L.

Rose-tinged waters break
Lilacs blossoming soft stars
uterine reprieve
waters burst through body's thirst
love past ache alive at last

dedicated to

Dr. Jennifer Ross

and to

Dr. Marilyn Milkman

11/3/96

HAIKU FOR b.b.L.

Lover help me love
New waves wash away my fears
Rain carry me home

POEM #9 FOR b.b.L.

I could as soon forget
about the wrapped-in newsprint
roses
As you could forget
(apparently all)
about me

KISSING GOD GOODBYE

Poem in the face of Operation Rescue

You mean to tell me on the 12th day or the 13th
that the Lord
which is to say some wiseass
got more muscle than he
reasonably
can control or figure out/ some
accidental hard disc
thunderbolt/ some
big mouth
woman-hating/ super
heterosexist heterosexual
kind of a guy guy
he decided who could live and who would die?

And after he did what?
created alleyways of death
and acid rain
and infant mortality rates
and sons of the gun
and something called the kitchenette
and trailer trucks to kill and carry
beautiful trees out of their natural
habitat/ Oh! Not that guy?

Was it that other guy
who invented a snake
an apple and a really
retarded scenario so that

down to this very day
it is not a lot of fun
to give birth to a son of a gun?
And wasn't no woman in the picture
of the Lord?
He done the whole thing by himself?
The oceans and the skies
and the fish that swim and the bird
that flies?

You sure he didn't have some serious problems
of perspective
for example
coming up with mountains/valleys/rivers/rainbows
and no companionship/no coach/no
midwife/boyfriend/girlfriend/
no help whatsoever for a swollen
overactive
brain
unable to spell
sex

You mean to tell me that the planet
is the brainchild
of a single
        male
        head of household?

And everything he said and done
the floods/famines/plagues
and pestilence
the invention of the slave and the invention of the gun
the worship of war (especially whichever war
he won)

And after everything he thought about and made 2 million
megapronouncements about
(Like)
"Give not your strength to women"
and
"You shall not lie with a male as with a woman"
and
"An outsider shall not eat of a holy thing"
and
"If a woman conceives and bears a male child
then she shall be unclean
seven days . . . But if she bears
a female child, then she shall be unclean
2 weeks . . ."
and
"The leper who has the disease
shall wear torn clothes and let the hair
of his head hang loose
and he shall cover his upper lip
and cry, " 'Unclean,
unclean!' "
and
"Behold, I have 2 daughters
who have not known a man,
let me bring them out to you, and do
to them as you please"
and
"I will greatly multiply your pain
in childbearing;
in pain shall you bring forth children"
and
"Take your son, your only son Isaac,
whom you love,
and go to the land of Moriah, and offer

him there as a burnt offering"
and in the middle of this lunatic lottery
there was Ruth saying to Naomi;
"Entreat me not
to leave you or to return
from following you; for where you go
I will go
and where you lodge I will lodge, your people
shall be my people
And your God my God;
where you die I will die,
and there I will be buried. May the Lord do so to me
and more also
if even death parts me from you."
and
David wailing aloud at the death of Jonathan who loved
      him
"more than his own soul" and David
inconsolable in lamentation
saying
". . . very pleasant have you been to me;
your love to me was wonderful,
passing the love of women"
and
"If I give away all I have, and if I deliver
my body to be burned,
but have not love,
I gain nothing . . ."
and this chaos/this chaos
exploded tyrannical in scattershot scripture
(Like)
". . . those who belong in Christ
Jesus have crucified the flesh
with its passions and desire"

and
"Cast out the slave and her son"
and
"If in spite of this you will not hearken
to me, then . . .
You shall eat the flesh of your sons,
you shall eat the flesh
of your daughters. And I will
destroy your high places . . . I will
lay your cities waste . . . I will
devastate your land . . . And
as for those of you that are left,
I will send faintness
into their hearts in the lands of their enemies
the sound of a driven leaf
shall put them to flight . . ."
etcetera etcetera
That guy?
That guy?
the ruler of all earth
and heaven too
The maker of all laws
and all taboo
The absolute supremacist
of power
the origin of the destiny
of molecules and Mars
The father and the son
the king and the prince
The prophet and the prophecy
The singer and the song
The man from whom
in whom
of whom

by whom
comes everything
without the womb
without that unclean
feminine
connection/
that guy?

The emperor of poverty
The czar of suffering
The wizard of disease
The joker of morality
The pioneer of slavery
The priest of sexuality
The host of violence
The Almighty fount of fear and trembling
That's the guy?
You mean to tell me on the 12th day or the 13th
that the Lord
which is to say some wiseass
got more muscle than he
reasonably
can control or figure out/some
accidental hard disc
thunderbolt/some
big mouth
woman-hating/super
heterosexist heterosexual
kind of a guy guy
he decided who could live and who would die?

And so
the names become
the names of the dead and the living
who love

Peter
John
Tede
Phil
Larry
Bob
Alan
Richard
Tom
Wayne
David
Jonathan
Bruce
Mike
Steve
And so
our names become
the names of the dead
and the living who love
Suzanne
Amy
Elizabeth
Margaret
Trude
Linda
Sara
Alexis
Frances
Nancy
Ruth
Naomi
Julie
Kate
Patricia

And out of that scriptural scattershot
our names become
the names of the dead

our names become
the names of the iniquitous
the names of the accursed
the names of the tribes of the abomination
because
my name is not Abraham
my name is not Moses/Leviticus/Solomon/Cain or Abel
my name is not Matthew/Luke/Saul or Paul
My name is not Adam
My name is female
my name is freedom
my name is the one who lives outside the tent of the father
my name is the one who is dark
my name is the one who fights for the end of the kingdom
my name is the one at home
my name is the one who bleeds
my name is the one with the womb
my name is female
my name is freedom
my name is the one the bible despised
my name is the one astrology cannot predict
my name is the name the law cannot invalidate
my name is the one who loves

and that guy
and that guy
you never even seen upclose

He cannot eat at my table
He cannot sleep in my bed
He cannot push me aside

He cannot make me commit or contemplate
    suicide

He cannot say my name
without shame
He cannot say my name
My name
My name is the name of the one who loves

And he
has no dominion over me
his hate has no dominion over me
I am she who will be free

And that guy
better not try to tell anybody about who
should live
and who should die
or why

His name is not holy
He is not my Lord
He is not my people
His name is not sacred
His name is not my name
His name is not the name of those who love the living

His name is not the name of those who love the living
and the dead

His name is not our name
we
who survive the death
of men and women

whose beloved
breath
becomes (at last)
our own

dedicated to Jennie Portnoff